First Edition 2025
10 9 8 7 6 5 4 3 2 1 0

Words, Photos & Graphics by
Superimposition (Quan)

Visual Soma
Non-Duality Art Collective

Published by
Mindless Books • Springvale
2025

www.mindlessbooks.com

Not There *Nor Here*

Superimposition

Mindless Books
2025

contents		
	1	the one
	2	nut
	3	washing
	4	bit
	5	game
	6	spheres
	7	ringtones
	8	contracts
	9	pot
	10	double-dealers
	11	heat
	12	bagman
	13	demons
	14	snacks
	15	architects
	16	waves
	17	epoxy
	18	solids
	19	packages
	20	cash
	21	vanity
	22	frogs
	23	nylon
	24	sssssssss
	25	ovoid
	26	saws
	27	rice
	28	reflected
	29	dust

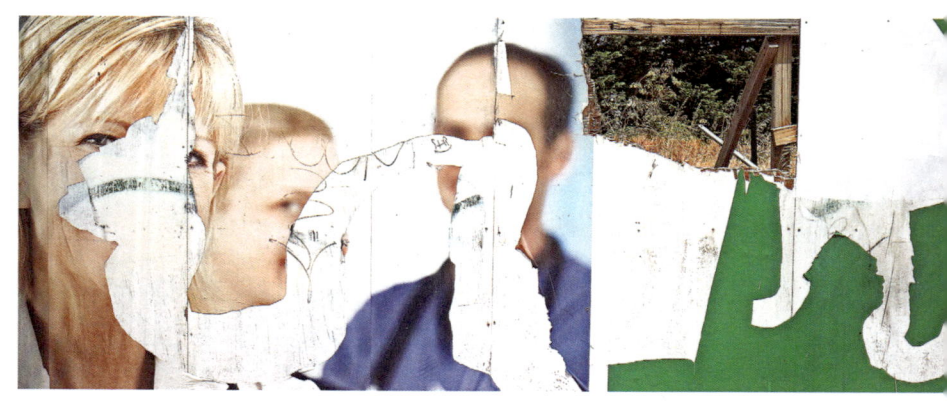

P R E
F A C E

a defect of the corn is to be loose and forgiving but
then installation hits and we wander into an exuberant
place of judgement not being pineapple mash aromatic
beyond your desired outlook for the coming quarter
so when you think it you do it but hey be pre-warned
to not leave have the items delivered to the local
operations manager there is a pink blanket to cover any
losses for when he comes out of the tele foxhole and
finds that it is overcooked we have no choice but to
spread out so thin it's undeserving of our attention in
time they made it for the enjoyers of satisfaction to turn
on the air conditioning and throw it in the volcano of
spices and the sparkling dots are destined for an array
of action sacks plotting against the one who knows
more than every position of impact let us go feed on
the assorted sweet berries before the snails gossip about
the new calendar format because the strokes are weak
although vibrant we need to insist that being together
is not practical for the forbidden who are left to nuture
the insensitive crowd that knows the purple moss
is alluring enough to warrant a deep and auspicious
mental plate as it's flung through the window only to
be edged out by the realm lords so when we think we
are ok to be around the soft but disjointed matter it
somewhat changes ok sure keep a fit body or lose sleep
whatever you decide make a good nest for it for it is
and it's nothing new really preventing the destructive
something to keep in mind you have the tools required
for they are to gobble the rules and a gnome will show
you where the next turn of the table is located perverse
we now colour outside the lines of perception this
naturally happens when there is no more…

nut a
biscuit
of urban
codes

filth inert
masquerading
over the top
they said parallel
to the washing
now once gone
the growth runs
as examples
told

arithmetic
unbuilt
the bit
&
mingle

frame
the song
crept up
game for
none
wrong lot
phobic

again by the kilo

it's distinct

the ceramic of spheres

*desolate
ringtones
numbers
traced and
transcended
with apparent
laced scones*

expanding contracts
A signwriting fact
the lettering tax

the not a pot
existence vomits
into a lot
an orange void
the track repeats
finding the stick
inconsistent

jcSh

*overfeeding
the elusive
double-dealers
we love the
crossbreeding
manifestation
loop*

speak
into
that
boiled
heat
please

bubbling to death the
magic bagman grinds
the bone

desire is unique

point less towards the
the circle

conjuring the drop of
emphasis

*emptiness predates an
observant fish between
moving demons and
the spectral gems
of the professional
interaction*

fghv

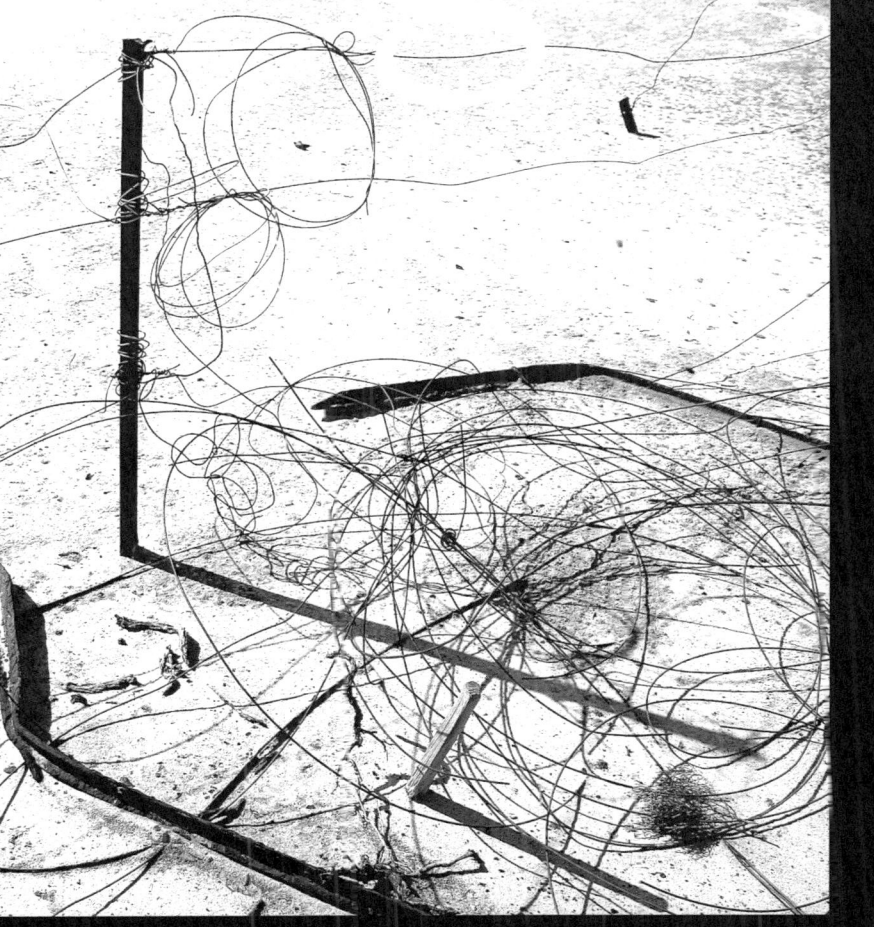

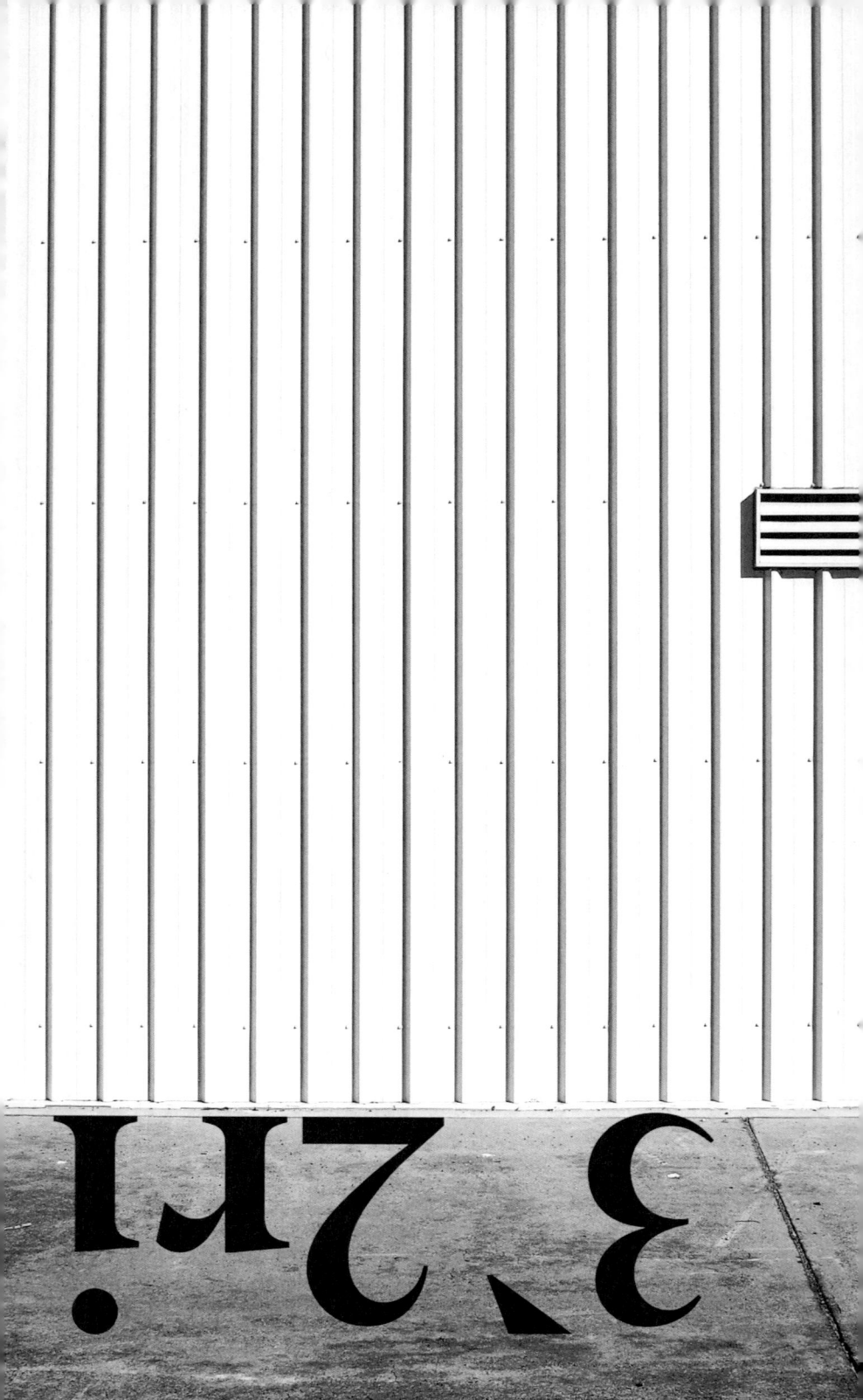

celestial
terror
a reminder

    the gifted
    demise of
      division

an
over supply
of snacks

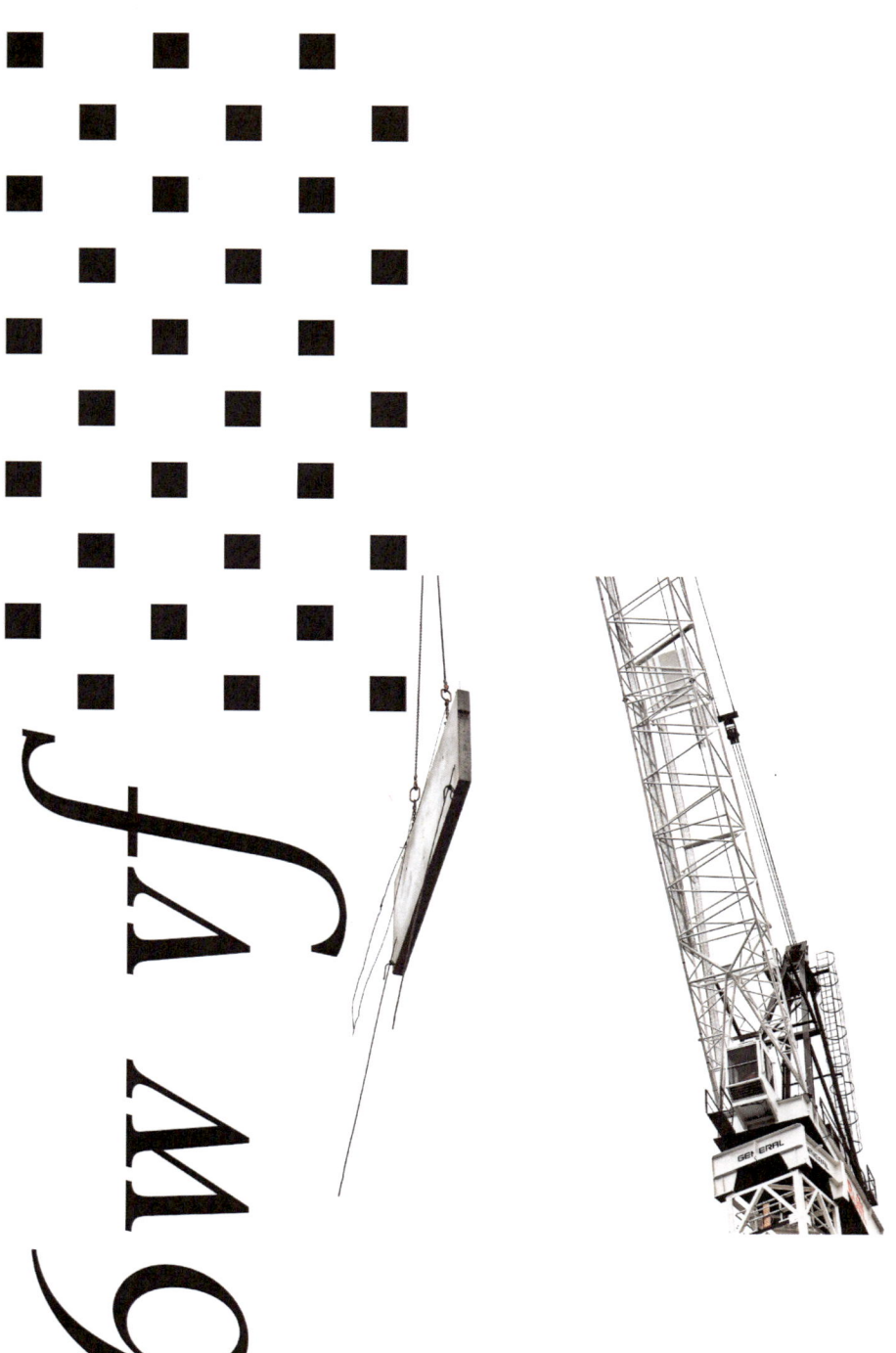

statistics
not desktop
architects
tricks the
empty clouds
as tone
disinfects

:[-'
=]O

sincerity would not allow
the waves cry
let us peel all the fruit
and stay

poking the
carrot of
sticks for an
epoxy grip
that clings to
gandantic
knots

XE%Q%$ES

a moving towards form
the thing to be dooming
insisting spiritualism

                                        solids stop
            but not arriving
until it leaves

*once ripe the
inner and outer
rejoice
now carry the
retrospect elf
and assorted
packages*

we are closed

m,fnf
o87gb
h

cash
to no
why
exit
where
to be

dispassionate audacity
contractual vanity
it moves without
a need or belief

the frogs
of solitude
pancake
rock the six
memories
of names
and fiscal

h45390835 8f
79b 4 1J
83925k
4;23ol;v-f0
\orw

wobble surgical
cubic pseudo
the nylon veil
belonging to
agnostic action

when
did it go?
um

no way!
SSSSSSSS

overt
meaning
over
thinking
ovoid

WHO

SEES

SAWS

uncooked rice

delight before the icons distort plurality

stop looking
said the reflected

dust imagined
a concrete thought
caught in the ride
they reappear
the spectators frown
an inaudible sound

KNO MOR

www.ingramcontent.com/pod-product-compliance
Lightning Source LLC
Chambersburg PA
CBRC092058200426
43209CB00068B/1871